Goodmoney
Collective

Goodmoney Collective

A chronicle of ATR:
A Territory Resource Foundation
which became the
Social Justice Fund Northwest

by Alan Rabinowitz

ISBN 978-1-4276-1664-7

Produced by Phil Kovacevich Design
with editiorial review by Sigrid Asmus

Printed in Canada
by Friesen's Book Manufacturers, Inc.

WRITTEN to interest every American citizen in helping the underprivileged and disenfranchised groups in our complex society to attain the equal and inalienable rights that the Universal Declaration of Human Rights says are the foundation of freedom, justice, and peace in the world.

DEDICATED to the wonderful troupe of members, staffers, board members, and grantees who joined with the founders of ATR in the last two decades of the 20th century to create a unique and enduring institution that would actually help such groups attain their rights.

A Territory Resource

Contents

Foreword

This biography is about ATR (officially A Territory Resource Foundation), a living, breathing, grantmaking "progressive charitable foundation" that has changed its name to Social Justice Fund Northwest and now has over 600 members in five states in the northwest part of the United States. ATR pioneered a kind of philanthropy that is effective, socially responsible, responsive, and emotionally satisfying to both the donors of dollars and to those who know how to put those dollars to good use. This book is one person's attempt at capturing the flavor of the innovative work of the hundreds of individuals who were its members, staff, grantees, and friends over the last three decades.

Our story begins in the late 1970s, when a small group of well-educated thirtyish idealists (many of whom had professional and graduate degrees), all from fairly affluent backgrounds, established a little charitable foundation to provide financial support to equally idealistic community-organizing projects in the Pacific Northwest. They believed their money, some earned in their professions but to a large extent inherited, was not only not "tainted" but was good, and that it could and should be used to make a better life for their communities. They believed in working collectively rather than in splendid isolation.

Almost everything about their venture was, in fact, innovative. They knew they wanted to be guided by experienced funders who understood "community." They were testing out new IRS rules for "public" rather than the usual "private" foundation. They wanted direct knowledge of their grantees and their challenges rather than merely writing checks for worthy causes. They wanted to encompass an ecological region rather than just one small locality. They were involved with ideas that were far more politically and spiritually progressive than were generally expected in the philanthropic community as it functioned in those days in their region. They hoped that many other people would become members of their group.

They did have trouble conjuring up a suitable name for this resource they were creating for their region and never could find anything better than A Territory Resource or ATR for short. As the years went by the context of the work changed in many ways, but just about everything they had hoped for came to pass, all as a result of hard work mixed with a great sense of discovery of self and of region and of the tricky business of giving money away with intelligence and with soul. After twenty-five years or so as ATR, a new generation took the reins and renamed it Social Justice Fund Northwest.

ATR, our pioneering collective of progressive donors, had its roots in the civil-rights and anti–Viet Nam passions of the 1960s and early 1970s, and it is hard for people who were not active then to realize that the feminist, environmental, and economic justice movements were then just underway, that the Native American, Latino-American and Asian-American groups were rarely included yet in the concept of minorities, that "gay pride" and AIDS were unknown terms, and that ATR's mission to support the empowerment of such disregarded, disadvantaged, and minority groups was a radical departure from traditional philanthropic practice.

ATR and Philanthropy Northwest, the regional association of grantmakers, are both about to celebrate their 30th birthdays. And it is fair to ask, Why are these organizations ONLY thirty years old instead of fifty or a hundred years old? To answer that question is to put the history of these philanthropic enterprises in the context of the series of democratizing transformations that constitute the birth, adolescence, and present status of the philanthropy sector of society as we know it today. Doing just that is the job of Chapter 1, but readers are welcome to omit that wind-up background material and jump right into Chapter 2 with its story of ATR's creation.

The word *pastiche* is a fair description of the rest of this essay. Added to my own memories and data happily offered from ATR's own dusty files are excerpts from well-written reports and ATR's intermittent newsletters. The excerpts are scattered throughout, providing contemporary viewpoints and considered reflections about the multifaceted activities of this unusual foundation.

My wife Andrea and I had the privilege of becoming members of ATR soon after it began, and I have tried to capture the spirit of those times in the pages that follow. While I want to honor all the hundreds of people who have devoted themselves to the work of ATR and its grantees, only a few names of principal actors on the scene will be found herein. A listing of the scores of members and community leaders who have served on the board of directors, plus a list of ATR's honorees, however, is to be found in Appendix One.

A truly adequate accounting of the accomplishments of the old ATR as it transmogrified itself into Social Justice Fund Northwest at the beginning of the 21st century must await a future chronicler, for the story presented here is primarily about life in the latter part of the 20th century. Admittedly a long round of interviews with the principal actors on the scene would serve the cause of capturing the spirit of this enterprise better than this short book; without such an effort, many important and unique stories about the life and times at ATR and SJFNW will surely remain untold, but such deep and thorough research has been beyond the resources available.

In any case, for what it is, enjoy this attempt to piece together an important and enlightening story.

CHAPTER 1

Context: Five decades of progressive philanthropy

The basic transformations that created the kind of philanthropic activity with which our society is familiar today began in the early years of the 20th century. At that time, America was deeply involved in the great task of empowering "the People" and of transitioning from decades of Social Darwinism, which was the dark side of Industrial Capitalism. Politically, that was the era of "good government" reforms, including the introduction of initiatives and referendums to let people have a direct voice in governance (with voting rights for women and Native Americans soon to follow).

Most philanthropy was of the traditional sort: gifts to hospitals and educational institutions and funding for religious charities, which still today comprise the bulk of giving in any year and cover contributions to churches and synagogues, missions (in what became known as the Third World after World War II), soup kitchens often run by missions to the homeless in the cities of America, cemeteries, and orphanages. And beyond those categories, secular philanthropy, with the exception of the major foundations that great industrialists such as Rockefeller, Carnegie, and Russell Sage had established at the end of the 19th century, was primarily associated with monuments memorializing wealthy patrons such as can be seen in New York in the American Museum of Natural History, the New York Public Library, the Metropolitan Museum of Art, Carnegie Hall, the Heye collection of Native American Art, and the Rockefellers' purchase of the Palisades Park as a present for the state of New York.

Such monumentalizing and memorializing activities were relatively scarce in the Northwest when the ATR foundation began its work in the 1970s. Only in the past few decades have major public improvements carried the names of individual donors. While a certain amount of traditional charity was seen in the western states back in the 1890s, Lord Bryce, whose great analysis of America's society and governance appeared at the ebullient end of the 19th century, observed that the Westerners who had made great fortunes in mining and timber felt that they were contributing as much to the commonweal as they needed to do if they built very large houses and indulged in other forms of conspicuous consumption designed to show the rest of the population that such riches were possible for everyone with a little work and a little luck. His observations certainly apply to parts of America in the 21st Century, as we write ATR's story.

Another major cultural transformation began to emerge some decades later, spurred by the idealism of the New Deal in contending with the social insecurities and displacements of the Great Depression, and by President Franklin D. Roosevelt's articulation of the Four Freedoms for which World War II was being fought: freedom of speech and expression, freedom to worship god as one chose; freedom from want, and freedom from fear. Then in the postwar period came Eleanor Roosevelt's stupendous achievement at the United Nations in getting the Universal Declaration of Human Rights adopted on December 10, 1948, followed by the equally remarkable blossoming of the civil rights and voting rights movements in the United States. The one-person one-vote ruling of the early 1960s brought still another needed aspect of democratization to our political system.

One branch of organized philanthropy became particularly energized as a result of the climate of idealism that was spurred by the UN's call for *recognition of . . . the equal and inalienable rights of all members of the human family is the foundation of freedom, justice, and peace in the world.* Taking the lead in creating what has come to be called social change philanthropy was the Stern Fund created by Edith Stern, an heir of the Sears Roebuck fortune. David Hunter was her executive director, and his oft-repeated and compelling belief was that true philanthropy is different from mere charity; he insisted that his brand of social change philanthropy had to be distinguished from run-of-the-mill philanthropy. *The essential difference,* he wrote, *is that social change philanthropy aims explicitly to facilitate the changing of societal institutions so they don't produce the very problems that "charity" tries to alleviate.*[1]

The basic concept that Hunter and the social change philanthropists were promoting was that grants needed to be provided to underprivileged and disenfranchised groups to enable them to get to be effective in the general society. Those of us in the related fields of community economic development and urban renewal came to understand and agree with this approach because good ideas and good leadership from the top were no longer carrying the day, just as today those in the global arena who are part of the World Trade Organization are having to learn the same lesson, to wit, that major changes of any kind, in order to be effective over the long run, require the real understanding and free consent of the people affected and need to be planned and implemented from the bottom up.

Hunter got a number of foundations as his allies in the late 1960s and early 1970s, including the Field Foundation, the DJB Foundation, and the Youth Project. He was not as successful in wooing the major foundations, but one of the biggies, the Ford Foundation, became activist in quasi-political ways on behalf of various progressive causes and candidates in the short-lived glory

1. Quoted from Hunter's foreword to Alan Rabinowitz, *Social Change Philanthropy in America* (Westport CT: Quorum/Greenwood, 1990), p. xi.

days of President Johnson's Great Society programs. Ford's grant-making stimulated the curiosity and, maybe more accurately, incurred the wrath of members of Congress, who launched an investigation into the hitherto occult world of the foundations. They did not approve of what Ford had been doing on the margins of politics, and they were appalled at what they discovered about the ways businessmen were using their little foundations for purposes that were more self-serving than public-serving. The result was the Tax Act of 1969 and, for the first time, a long list of commandments for the structure and operation of organizations that wished to preserve their exemption from federal income taxation.

While the liberal, progressive segment of society was learning to appreciate and encourage those who were being disempowered or forgotten by the economy or unfairly affected by the Viet Nam war, the far right was also organizing to show that they were more patriotic, more moral, more independent and entrepreneurial than those on the left. In the 1964 campaign, Goldwater fired the opening shots. Nixon and his troupe of Westerners and Southerners, helped by George Wallace and his brand of supporters, finally captured the presidency in 1968. The split between the right and the left has simply gotten wider decade after decade since then.

The struggle between right and left was partly caused by important and rather fundamental changes that were going on in the American economy and thus in its philanthropic practices during the entire post–World War II period. During the War, income tax rates had risen dramatically to cover wartime expenses (in contrast to the reluctance of Presidents Reagan and Bushes I and II to raise taxes for their starwars and earthwars, and who preferred to drown the U.S. in deficits instead). Because tax rates were not expected to return to the low prewar levels, a variety of businessmen and their families began to establish little charitable foundations into which they could plow money that could stay in their foundation's coffers and be exempt from federal taxes. They and their friends constituted the board, often with salaries to boot. They could use the assets to support all sorts of individuals and often-but-not-always worthy causes, and they could also invest the capital back into the business in the form of loans or ownership of their business facilities. All of the above activities were indisputably legal (and sometimes actually philanthropic) under the rules then prevailing in the ebullient economic expansion of the postwar period.

During this same post–World War II period the more responsible parts of the philanthropic community began to feel the need for some order out of the developing chaos. The present-day Council on Foundations (COF) states that its precursor was started in 1949 as an informal collection of community foundations, community chests, and major social-service organizations such as the YMCA and the Boy Scouts. Next, in 1956, a few major foundations established The Foundation Center as an information resource for the public. Several years later the organization that became the Council on Foundations was incorporated, and soon private and company foundations were admitted as affiliate members; full membership was not extended to corporate and family foundations until 1964. Then, according to the history on the Council's Web site:

> *Shock waves go through the foundation field as the result of hearings and other legislative activity leading to passage of the Tax Reform Act of 1969, which, for the first time levies serious restrictions on private foundations including: (1) an excise tax on investment income, (2) a minimum payout requirement, (3) certain limitations on charitable gifts to foundations, and (4) penalties for such activities as self-dealing and excess business holdings.*

Quite possibly neither the philanthropy field nor the U.S. Congress has ever recovered from the shock of transforming the field as required by the Tax Act of 1969. In the ensuing years, a continual process of self-evaluation by the philanthropic establishment began with the five-volume Filer Commission report issued in 1975. The next year, continues the COF history, the board adopted "a Resolution on Foundations and Social Justice." At the same time, some skeptical philanthropists supported the creation of the National Committee for Responsive Philanthropy (NCRP) to be a watchdog over the philanthropic industry and an enthusiast for the Filer Commission's vision. The actual extent to which organized philanthropy in America has succeeded in enhancing social justice as David Hunter and his colleagues defined it might be a fine topic for a future dissertation in one of the graduate programs in philanthropy that began to appear at the end of the 20th century.

To transform the field in Hunter's terms first mandates a change in the relation between grantor-donor-funder and grantee-donee-fundee. Social change philanthropy, almost by definition and manifestly by practice, involves "effective communication" between (a) the proposed grantee and (b) the program officer of a foundation or a generous individual (who may be masked by doing his/her work through a family foundation or a donor-advised account).

A second required change is in the nature of the grantee that the funder is willing to deal with. Still today for most foundations, a prospective grantee has to be well-established, with solid citizens on its board, already reasonably well-supported financially by a constituency, and fiscally responsible. The typical social change grantee is much smaller and is energized by a worthy cause, but is administratively fragile and financially weak, and is trying to organize a group of people unused to organized politicking for redress of grievances. In most cases the staff and officers of the social change grantee are unfamiliar with the heady atmosphere of the institutions, foundations, and well-situated individuals who are rallying to their cause by means of the grantmaking process.

A third change necessarily had to take place in the grantmaking community itself. The Tax Act of 1969, of course, had taken hold, providing fairly clear rules for starting and operating nonprofit entities and foundations and moderating their involvement in legislation and elections. The more traditional foundations continued their focus on funding hospitals, schools and universities, boys and girls clubs, soup kitchens, and the panoply of organizations of the type favored by the United Ways of the nation. But the concept was spreading to the effect that the well-to-do should also be helping the emerging group of community-level and grassroots activities, and out of the societal agitations of the '60s came the new "public" foundations provided for in the 1960 Tax Act, no different in law from the more familiar community foundations but somewhat unsettling to the traditional leaders of the philanthropic world.

A leading example of this new form was The Youth Project, a pioneer in the funding of progressive community-activist organizations and a training ground for both those who established donor-advised accounts and for staff members who went on to become staff of countless other activist groups and foundations. The Youth Project set the tone for a generation of young, well-to-do people in their twenties and thirties who had spent years being inspired and educated by the social upheavals of the late 1960s and early 1970s.

Some heirs of the Pillsbury fortune started a coterie of such public foundations in the mid-seventies: Haymarket in Boston, Liberty Hill in Los Angeles, and Vanguard in San Francisco, soon joined by North Star in New York City, MRG/McKenzie River Gathering in Eugene, Oregon, and a dozen others around the country. They went on to publish *Robin Hood Was Right*,[2] a delightful book that became one of the great guides in this new era in charitable giving. The political dogma of this coterie was that the duty of donors was to make their financial contribution and then, as a gesture of giving up their power to direct their gifts, get out of the way while representatives of the grassroots world of the disempowered made culturally and politically relevant grants to qualified groups in their locale. The Funding Exchange was created to facilitate relationships among this score of unendowed public foundations who lived from year to year by soliciting small and large contributions from their members. The founders of A Territory Resource never agreed that it was either wise or necessary to give up their individual power; far better to have donor and grantee learn to work and live together.

2. Originally published in 1977 by the Vanguard Public Foundation, now available from W. W. Norton (New York, 2000).

CHAPTER 2

The creation of A Territory Resource Foundation

Enter not only the spirit of David Hunter but the man himself. He became the mentor for the handful of young adults who banded together to form A Territory Resource Foundation (ATR), a small public foundation dedicated to the practice of social change philanthropy for its chosen territory, the five Northwestern states where its original members lived: Washington, Oregon, Montana, Idaho, and Wyoming. Hunter was impressed that ATR's funder-members wanted to deal with their own feelings about having money, that they needed to meet and understand their grantees and the grantees' issues, and that the grantees needed to know and understand (or at least have some empathy for) their funders. ATR has thus never been entitled to join the Funding Exchange because it could not subscribe to the dogma of separating donor and donee.

The first edition of *Robin Hood Was Right: A Guide for Giving Your Money for Social Change*, as published by the Vanguard Public Foundation in 1977, quickly created a common language for scores of well-to-do young people who were looking for constructive ways to deal with their fortunes. At a meeting at Asilomar on the California coast, one of many convenings that were arranged by progressive social change activists, including the creators of Vanguard Foundation, to attract more such privileged young people into the fold, some Northwestern and Northern Rockies individuals got to know each other and thought about next steps. We have reproduced below the gingerly worded invitation that went out in early 1978 for a follow-up meeting in Seattle. Its text is redolent with all of the emotional considerations to be dealt with by fledgling philanthropists.

> *HISTORY: This meeting is an outgrowth of a gathering this spring in California of a group of young people with the common problem of dealing with inherited wealth and the common desire to use it to effect social change. A few of us who were new to the group discussed the desire to have a regional meeting so others could share in a similar experience and we could continue the positive energy the gathering had generated for us. Also we were hoping that this meeting will be an opportunity for us to begin exploring ways of funding projects of common interest in the Northwest.*
>
> *I have pulled together the outline below from my personal interests using the format for the meeting this spring as a guide. We need not follow it if discussions lead elsewhere. It is merely a suggestion and a structure to fall back on. I would like the meeting to be as spontaneous as possible.*

SATURDAY, JUNE 4

10 am   *INTRODUCTION – GETTING ACQUAINTED*
    Topic: Personal History – Attitudes toward Inheritance –
    Positive and Negative Experiences
        Some questions we can discuss:
        How do you deal with money and friends?
        How do you say 'No'?

LUNCH

        AFTERNOON
        Topic: Giving
        Some questions we can discuss:
                How do you make decisions on what to fund?
                What categories are you interested in
                    funding in the Northwest?
                Are you interested in exploring methods of
                    establishing a foundation in the
                    Northwest patterned after Haymarket
                    in Boston, Vanguard in San Francisco,
                    or Liberty Hill in Los Angeles?
            Please bring information on:
                Groups in the Northwest seeking funding;
                Foundations, etc., which we could use as models.

BREAK FOR VOLLEYBALL

        Optional topic: Investment policies
        Some questions we can discuss:
                How important is it to have a clean portfolio?
                Have you ever made venture capital investments?
                Was it satisfactory?

*DINNER at a Chinese restaurant or whatever for whoever
is not "talked out."*

SUNDAY, JUNE 5

10:30 am   BRUNCH
> *Continuing discussion for those interested in
> pursuing a foundation.*
> *Some questions we should address:*
>> *What are our common goals to be used as
>> criteria in funding?*
>> *What fields are we interested in funding?*
>> *What foundation models do we favor –
>> community and/or donor involvement in the
>> decision process?*
>> *When and where should our next meeting be?*

The meeting did happen and produced a group long recognized as
"The Founders of A Territory Resource," composed of the following: Alice Bristow (an alias), Mary Brumder and her husband Ebo
Teichmann, Jill Bullitt, Max Milton, and Connie Staudohar with
her husband Chris Boyd. There were good reasons why one of that
group (listed here as Alice Bristow) always wished to remain com-
pletely anonymous; an abiding fear on the part of young people
with money is that they will be taken advantage of by friends,
employers, stockbrokers, media reporters, and all sorts of unsavory
characters. These concerns were reflected in the very first topic for
the founding meeting, and the same need for confidentiality and
trust is invariably emphasized at the beginning of any get-together

of fledgling philanthropists. As Max Milton wrote in the ATR newsletter twenty years later:

> *Most of us were uncomfortable being identified as a part of the ownership class that was perceived as perpetuating social inequities. We worked alongside social activists and did not want the inevitable separation, publicity and unending appeals for money which came with being identified as wealthy. We wanted to work together, pooling our resources and knowledge of issues to create better funding. We chose the Pacific North West as our focus because we live here and because of a common concern about coal strip mining.*
>
> . . .
>
> *In the early ATR days, the safety, support and anonimity of our collaboration as "donors in training" was as important to our purpose for being as our funding. Many of our families were frequently indifferent to our work; some were actively hostile. We were novices making up new rules of philanthropy to suit our purposes. We made great friendships and had a lot of fun!*

Out of one of those early meetings came the name, A Territory Resource, and a tradition of song. A version of Woody Guthrie's "Roll On Columbia" emerged as the anthem, with ditties about each new member being added as the years rolled on. Here, without the repetitive chorus, is some of the doggerel, which actually tells more about those intense months than any text we could write:

This is the story of how we began
On the beach at Asilomar: Jill, Max, and [Alice]
Promised to meet in Seattle with a plan
To roll over Northwest . . . Roll o'er Northwest . . . etc.

[David Hunter] rolls into meetings and sometimes is quiet
But behind that facade he's plotting a riot
Funding the radicals is his daily diet.
So roll on, David, roll on . . .

Peace and disarmament is what he works for,
So he sends us mass mailings each day to our door,
We read and we read so he sends us ten more

A call to David sent Heather to stay.
With luck she directed Mary our way.
Little did she know the part she'd play
To roll over Northwest . . .

Flat on her back lay Mary . . .
In walked Max, no last name had he,

Chris and Connie ate pizza for ration
In darkness as their first initiation . . .

Into the picture came Nancy and Wink,
No introductions, just "what do you think?"
One vote for two people, how rinky-dink!

Said Alice, "a foundation is certainly our key
To roll over Northwest . . .

It seemed impossible to choose a name.
Should it be Nettles, Chinook, or Rain?
Thus by default ATR it became
So roll on, ATR, roll on

The banquet had songs, we all ate our fill,
Then Twist and Shout was belted out by Jill.
Max awarded an award, he's presenting it still, so
Roll on, ATR, roll on

Two of the founders were born in the Northwest. The others and most of the members recruited in the early years came from cities thousands of miles to the east, with a smaller lot southerly from California and Oregon. By August 1978, not long after this first meeting in June, the founders each contributed substantial sums to a pot of money to be distributed after due deliberation to an appropriate and acceptable docket of grantees, and they held the first annual meeting of their brand-new and manifestly unendowed public foundation. This decision required them to become a much larger group to satisfy the IRS's conditions for the public foundation designation, since the tax exemption for the necessary annual donations to public foundations was more generous than donations to private foundations. Accordingly they recruited new members, doubling the size of the group within the year and doubling it again within a few more years to fifteen to twenty members, a size that seemed to all the participants quite large enough for awhile. In those days, a full annual membership contribution for an individual was $3,500.

A foundation is a corporation that needs directors and officers who are willing to have their names on public records. Mary Brumder was the designated founder able and willing to go public and act as president; not until about 1985 were any other donors given seats on the board. The other board members were all experienced activists: the redoubtable David Hunter from the Stern Fund in New York; Heather Booth from her Midwest Academy in Chicago; and Bill Mitchell, deputy director of the Youth Project in Washington, DC. Kim Clerc, a senior community organizer at Oregon Fair Share in Portland, and Michael Fox, a progressive lawyer in Seattle, were soon added to the list of directors. More of Max Milton's recollections:

> *Another strong focus came from our early advisory board, which we chose to mentor us, on what effective social change looked like and how it might come about. The group of experienced funders, citizen organizers and community organizers shared with us the advantages and disadvantages of various models and strategies. We decided to concentrate our funding on community based citizen organizations which, if nurtured, would create a constituency for progressive social policy.*
>
> . . .
>
> *The threat of massive strip mining of coal in the interior West to feed the growing energy needs of the rapidly urbanizing coastal states was one of the most contentious issues of the time. Energy strategies of the day had potentially disastrous consequences. Native Americans and ranchers were threatened with displacement. Rural areas would suffer financial hardship. And massive air pollution would be created.*

Next order of business was to hire someone to assist in the work of putting a docket together, keeping the corporation legally operational, and working with Mike Fox, who was serving as both treasurer and legal counsel for the group; Mike was a lawyer in Seattle with an exciting record in organizing unions for farmworkers (he would eventually become a judge). The someone who got hired turned out to be the wrong person; she had neither experience nor interest in the array of social problems with which the founding members wished to deal, and, more importantly, she did not think that the individual members, each one fairly well-to-do and well educated, should be meeting face-to-face with grantees in the fashion that seemed necessary to the members if they were to understand the needs of the prospective grantees and have those grantees begin to understand them as grantors. She was shortly replaced with Greg Caplan'Tuke, a young social worker, born in Spokane and endowed with a rare set of assets—enthusiasm for social action, the ability to listen and learn along with the members, and a love of music and athletics that energized ATR's corporate life and helped meld the membership into an effective organization.

By then being a member of ATR in its formative years was lots of fun, emotionally challenging, demanding of time and money, and offering unequaled and vast opportunities for discovering fabulous reaches of the Northwest. Its grantmaking was exciting, for ATR was a pioneering funder of the region's environmental movement, of its feminist and GLBT (gay, lesbian, bisexual, and transgender) groups, especially as AIDS became rampant in the U.S., and of the new breed of multi-issue and single-issue organizations across the region. We learned a great deal about the work and about ourselves in the period when ATR had no more than twenty to thirty members and when all its meetings involved close interactions between members and a small board composed almost exclusively of community organizers and other experienced philanthropoids plus the inimitable David Hunter.

The whole idea quickly coalesced with a mixture of fun and serious attention to the work, with grantmaking and educational meetings scheduled during the school year (while most of the members were dealing with regular jobs and many with quite small children), and the summer conclaves when members from the five states came together for three or four days to discover new parts of the fabulous northwestern environment and to enjoy hot tubs, river rafting, dancing, and the exquisite angsts of policy making. The first out-of-Seattle summer meeting was in 1979 at Chico Hot Springs Lodge, Pray, Montana. The next year's conclave was at Hall's Resort, Priest Lake, Idaho, and in 1980 at Bridger Mountain Lodge in Montana. Always invited to the summer meetings were spouses, significant others, children, and a wide variety of local and state-level politicians, community organizers, and experts in the issues to be discussed.

Greg Caplan'Tuke worked manfully at the manifold tasks of being executive director of a group that had more chiefs than indi-ans (the kind of expression that was abhorred by a membership that was overwhelmingly antiracist), and he learned to weave art-fully and cheerfully between the overlordship of the corporation's books—exercised on an almost daily basis by Mary—and the daily detailed critiques and contributions to the work in hand by Alice. Alice deserves much of the credit for the consistently illuminating graphics that graced ATR's various publications at the time, and Greg can be credited for initiating most of the innovative activities for which ATR became known. Before long, ATR issued its first for-mal status report to cover the initial 1978–1980 period, with intro-ductory text by Greg, as excerpted below.

> *A Territory Resource (ATR), since its inception
> in 1978, has become an important part of the fund-
> ing network in the Northwest/Northern Rockies . . .*

In addition to grant-making, ATR has increased its technical assistance to groups in the region. Supporting workshops on leadership development and providing direct assistance to groups doing fundraising have been two primary areas of focus. In addition, ATR has encouraged national activists to come to the region and to share their experience and knowledge.

ATR's grant-making has moved from focusing on particular issue areas such as Energy and Women to focusing more on the strategies to be used by organizations in furthering their work. Strategies that build long-lasting organizations which give participants a sense of control over their lives have been the primary focus. Overall ATR has developed a clearer strategy and a more active role for itself in this region.

At this point, Greg provided some statistics that demonstrate this progress during ATR's first two and a half years. Table 1 lists the grants by name, and the reader is welcome to imagine how each member was induced to read each grant proposal and be prepared to discuss the pros and cons of making any grant at all and then be willing to argue more or less passionately for a given dollar amount for the grant. Figure 1 is Alice Barstow's diagram of ATR's procedure for reconciling individual views as to the acceptability of specific projects.

Part of the fun was engaging in spirited debate about the appropriateness and possible effectiveness of each grant. Sadly, the particularity of the process faded considerably as the volume of grants expanded over the years and as the bureaucratic demand for orderliness in the process began ineluctably to limit the involvement of even the most eager member. By the end of the century, just a listing of the grants for a year could induce mental overload.

A good-sized book could be written about this list of grantees, for they constitute a blue-ribbon collection that is truly representative of progressive causes at the beginning of the eighties. A few of them are noted in the lengthy appendix to the study by Mike Clark discussed in the next chapter.

FIGURE 1. ATR's grantmaking procedure in 1980

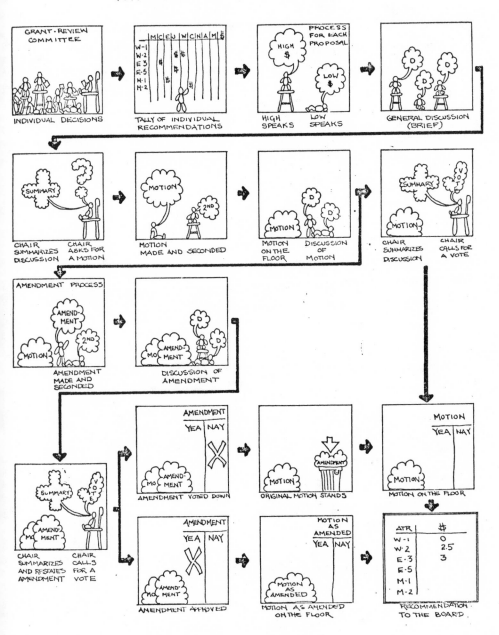

In recent years, the grant amount is more or less predetermined and probably falls into a certain category, $5,000 for this category, $10,000 for that category, no exceptions, up or down. In the early days the grant amounts were smaller, as seen in Table 1, and the granting decision turned on whether the grantee should get $3,750 or $3,500 and what kind of a process should we have to settle the matter? And, of course, each grant had to be screened in relation to the total amount available for granting at that time. In any case, the members were proud to present their 1978–1980 records to the public.

TABLE 1. Grants 1978–1980

Grants 1978–1980

August 1978

Citizen/Labor Energy Project	$5,000
Bitterroot Educational Resources for Women	$1,000
Neighborhood Rape Relief – Outreach Project	$1,000
Seattle Working Women	$2,000
Violence Against Women Project	$1,000
Cherry Hill Coalition	$1,500
Northwest Labor and Employment Law Office	$2,500

June 1979

Agriculture and Public Resources Project	$5,000
Local Energy Organizers Project	$4,000
Northern Tier Pipeline Project	$3,000
Northwest Indian Women's Council	$2,000
Seattle Working Women	$3,000
Regional Forums	($1,500)
Northwest Immigration Alliance Project	$ 500
Organizing Project	$4,960

November 1979

Lifeline Organizing Project	$1,500
Light Brigade's Tacoma/Snohomish Organizing Project	$5,000
Organizing new constituencies of Rural and Farm Women	($3,443)
Montana Co-op Project	$5,000
Chicana/Latina Research Project	$2,000
Coalition on Government Spying	$1,500

February 1980

Montana Pro-Choice Coalition	$4,500
Washington Coalition of Sexual Assault Programs	$1,230
Oregon Energy Project	$5,000
Uranium Project	$3,280

November 1980

Idaho Fairshare Start-up	$4,000
Northwest Energy Project	$2,000
Northwest Organizing Project	$5,000
One for One Busing	$2,000
Plant Closings Educational Outreach	$2,500
Southern Oregon Organizing Project	$5,000
Management Training for Community Organizers	$1,000

In Table 2, the left-hand columns show how the contributions mounted slowly year by year, the larger share coming from the Puget Sound area and mostly in larger amounts than the minimum membership fee. And although the grant amounts in the right-hand columns appear small by 21st century standards, they were significant sums to the recipients, most of whom had little access to major donors of any sort. All this activity occurred while Jimmy Carter was in the White House. The political climate for social change philanthropy would shortly thereafter become more difficult to deal with under President Reagan and his successors.

TABLE 2. Contributions received and grants paid, 1978–1980

CONTRIBUTIONS			GRANTS		
By Year	No.	Amount	No.*	Amount	Average Size
1978	4	33,086	7	14,000	2,000
1979	28	53,064	14	42,403	3,000
1980	28	77,030	11	35,510	3,200
1978–80	60	$163,180	32	$91,913	$2,900
By State					
Regionwide	–	–	4	17,000	4,300
Idaho	0	0	2	7,443	3,700
Montana	7	32,913	6	18,500	3,100
Oregon	3	3,200	4	13,500	3,400
Washington	25	96,104	15	32,190	2,200
Wyoming	1	3,014	1	3,280	3,280
Out of region	24	27,949	–		
By Issue					
Energy	–		9	33,780	3,800
Women	–		12	27,673	2,300
Organizing	–		9	26,460	2,900
Miscellaneous	–		2	4,000	2,000
By Amount					
$ 000–$2,999	38	14,977	17	26,730	1,600
$3,000–$5,000	9	30,859	15	65,183	4,300
Over $5,000	13	117,344	–		

* including two in 1979 that did not work out, with grant monies returned.

The little sums tabulated at the left became dwarfed by the same kind of statistics in later years, as the number and range of grantees expanded and as the style of the grantmaking process became far more complex, given the larger number of members and other contributors to a much larger pot of money to give away. The staff also wrote a full-dress 37-page Progress Report covering the foundation's initial 1978–1980 period. The report began with the dramatic discovery that *we are now faced with how to continue funding in a responsible and reliable way* and continued with a running commentary (from report pages 27–28) of the issues or problem areas they had been funding.

> *We all take the responsibility of having money seriously. We recognize the inequities that surround us and want to use our money to change this. We also realize that the funds we have will be hardly more than a drop in the bucket and that we must concentrate our funding in order to have an effect.*
>
> *In focusing our grant-making we were able to clarify three other underlying philosophies that unite us. We recognize that change occurs slowly. We don't expect it to happen overnight. Therefore, we review projects in the context of their long-range goals and whether they are building a structure that will last.*

The Progress Report is a splendid document, but, after five more years of the kind of activity it described, the members wanted a reasonably dispassionate (and thus pioneering) evaluation of ATR's significance and effectiveness, so they commissioned Mike Clark, known to many of them as an experienced community organizer and who was then working in Colorado, to interview their grantees and draw whatever conclusions emerged thereby; the conclusions are discussed in Chapter 3 below. Such disinterested evaluations are still uncommon in the field.

ATR logo circa 1978

CHAPTER 3

The first look backward toward the future

ATR did indeed take itself and its work seriously as the constituencies with which it dealt began to suffer from the policies instituted by the Reagan team. ATR had become a well-functioning outfit. It was a relatively halcyon time within ATR for the larger number of members who, together with a flock of children and a variety of spouses, contributed not only money but a wide range of talents. Completing the mix were additional directors and office staff orchestrated by Greg Caplan'Tuke as executive director, imaginative grantsman, expert on community organizing and social action, general factotum, and master of ceremonies.

But the question always in the back of the collective mind at ATR was whether all the funding and all the dynamic relations between funder and fundee were making any difference for the causes or for the region. And so the directors sponsored a pioneering bit of research to explore that question. It was unique at the time in its attempt to listen to what the grantees would not otherwise have felt comfortable talking about with the providers of money they needed to run their organizations, and in its willingness to go public with what a truly independent research consultant discovered. The person they hired to do the job was Mike Clark, a seasoned organizational development specialist in the Rocky Mountain West. An ATR Planning Committee was established; Greg Caplan'Tuke's new successor Dave Bockmann acted as Clark's contact with the foundation. Mike's formal report was published as *Soundings: A Regional Survey of A Territory Resources' Grantees* in September 1985.

Clark set out to survey the current needs of ATR grantees and to make some recommendations for future ATR funding activities and programmatic work in its five-state region. His report was based on a series of telephone interviews and twenty follow-up personal visits with the managers of groups funded by ATR during the 1979–1985 period. His conclusions were an amalgam of their responses so that no individual respondent could be identified, and his appendix was an array of quotations that "seemed to be particularly insightful, enlightening, or entertaining."

Of course, much of what he learned was music to ATR's collective ear. ATR, he reported, is unique among social change groups in the region in that it is an invaluable funding source and a "key intellectual resource and technical assistance center, especially for young, emerging groups." And, of great importance to ATR's concept of itself, he continued:

> *By funding new groups and projects, it often can legitimize an issue or an organization. This process often enhances the ability of groups to successfully raise funds from other sources.*
>
> . . .
>
> *As a stable, regional institution, ATR is uniquely positioned to play a crucial leadership role among activists in the region. For this to take place, ATR must continue to be sensitive to issues of accountability toward both its donors and the constituency of social change groups it has created over the years.*
>
> . . .
>
> *The degree of trust exhibited toward ATR by most grantees is extraordinarily high and appears to be the result of several years of hard work by both ATR board and staff.*

And he could not avoid reporting how the policies of the Reagan administration were affecting the activities of the grantees he interviewed:

> *Within just five years, the Reagan Administration has created enormous shifts in public policy and in the public's view of how government should function. . . . Within this context, effective organizing styles and strategies are still emerging . . .*
>
> *ATR's list of grantees demonstrates the diversity and scope of social change groups within the region. The list includes peace groups, women's organizations, groups working on racial problems, environmental groups, multi-issue neighborhood groups, statewide coalitions dealing with political reform, and groups attempting to carry out economic development activities. Most are urban based but a sizeable number have a rural focus. . . . Almost all have been influenced by organizing styles developed out of two waning national movements: labor organizing and civil rights. . . . In general, the groups share a common concern for empowerment of citizens on a local level.*
>
> . . .
>
> *As the Reagan Administration has successfully altered longstanding public policies dealing with social services, the environment, national defense, etc., many national foundations have also shifted their funding priorities. Often, these changes have put largely rural regions with dispersed populations at a severe disadvantage in competing for grants. In an increasingly competitive contest for limited funds,*

*public interest groups in ATR's funding region face
serious impediments in gaining access to national
private foundations.*

. . .

*Many national foundations have drawn back from
issue areas that were popular in the Seventies.
Environmental groups may not be as popular with
funders as they were a few years ago. The same could
be said for other issues, such as women's rights and
poverty.*

Many of Mike Clark's findings and comments were unsurprising
but had rarely been documented in the field. To today's sophisti-
cated observers they might seem trite; at the time they seemed
profound and even original, certainly thoughtful and useful for
planning future strategies. For example, he found general agree-
ment that regional gatherings might be useful although there was
no consensus on the direction a regional conference might take; in
any case, the costs of sponsoring such a gathering would be prohib-
itive. Naturally he discovered that most of ATR's grantees had
endemic financial problems.

■ *Some will not survive in their current form; major changes
will be necessary in their programs and in their fund raising
efforts if they are to last through this decade. Some may dis-
appear within the next two years.*

■ *While some groups give lip service to regional issues, there is
no great value currently placed upon regional work by most
grassroots groups and statewide organizations . . . unless the
session has a clear focus on their particular issues.*

■ *There is considerable unease among the more experienced*

leaders about the consequences of ATR assuming an educational role in the region. Foundations – through their ability to provide or withhold funds – can drastically influence the nature of organizations and movements. While ATR is seen as an organization that is sensitive to these concerns – many grantees believe that the initiatives for programs in the region should come from grantees rather than funders . . .

■ *Many grantees are also concerned that any efforts to launch new activities at ATR might drain energy and resources away from ATR's vital role of funding effective groups within the region. This is a particularly strong concern among people who have maintained close contacts with ATR over the years. . . . They question whether or not ATR should attempt to assume new responsibilities outside of its traditional role of funding social change groups.*

■ *This region has attracted sizeable amounts of private foundations' money for social change issues. It is unlikely to do so in the future unless new advocacy efforts for the region take place.*

■ *[F]oundation proposal deadlines end up as the major factor in setting programmatic goals and time frames for operating programs . . .*

More subtle than the funding problems were the administrative and personnel issues which are *still* difficult for grantmakers to accept but which Mike Clark found to be equally endemic:

■ *Most activists quickly find that there are limited career opportunities available to them which can provide adequate professional challenges and financial rewards. One result is a small, highly active core of young staff members and a rapidly growing number of young and middle-aged former activists who are still deeply committed to social change but who see no means of maintaining full-time, or even part-time, involvement with citizen groups. Perhaps this "graying" of Sixties activists and "forced retirement" of even younger organizers is a natural consequence of how decentralized social change movements develop in our society. Even so, to accept the phenomenon as inevitable ensures the loss of skills and insights gained by large numbers of people through hard work on progressive causes over the past twenty years. It may continue to be impossible for many people to find paid work within the social change field, but the potential for applying the skills of a large number of experienced but relatively inactive organizers should be more consciously addressed.*

- *A few years ago it was feasible to argue that if an organization could obtain some seed funds and define a clear mission, there was a high probability that funds would eventually become available. That is no longer the case. It is possible to develop a highly useful program over the years and discover that the pot of social change money is simply not ample enough to support all of the groups now clamoring for funds . . .*

- *Almost three-fourths of the groups surveyed had experienced a change in staff leadership in the past few years. . . . A variety of explanations are offered for this rapid turnover but much of it comes down to four key factors: low wages, extremely high expectations of performance from both board and staff, lack of career opportunities within the citizen's movement, and the overwhelming complexity and scale of the problems most groups chose to challenge. One other important factor should be noted – the accumulative impact of dealing with a national administration whose policies run counter to the fundamental values and assumptions of ATR-funded citizen groups.*

- *In a region as vast as ATR's, delivery of competent technical assistance to grassroots groups is an extremely difficult task. It becomes even more difficult in times of tight money.*

- *Around the region, there is growing reliance upon staff members who are recent immigrants to the region. . . . more efforts are needed to identify and nurture native leaders in the region.*

The Clark report was available in draft form at the ATR annual meeting in the summer of 1985 and was essential reading for everyone as the discussion turned to the concept that ATR's grants for organizing and supporting the building of a progressive movement in the Northwest would be meaningful only to the extent that the five state legislatures contained a goodly number of strongly progressive leaders.

CHAPTER 4

Creating the Western States Center to help build a progressive movement in the Northwest

As the 1985 ATR summer meeting began, no one at ATR was fully aware of the fact that the right wing was launching an onslaught on the culture of progressives that would continue for more than twenty years, at least to the end of the George W. Bush administration in 2008. Coincidentally at that 1985 meeting, however, the members undertook a long review of the situation with Karen Thomas, an ATR director and expert in organizational matters, as facilitator, and they reached consensus that ATR would never have the staff or the time to do all the convening, research, and other work required to help build a true movement and that, therefore, some separate but allied organization was needed to implement useful research-based ideas that were logistically far beyond ATR's capabilities.

That fall, a few of ATR's major donor-members decided to follow up the summer meeting by creating what would ultimately be named the Western States Center. They raised a fund to cover basic first-year expenses. They asked Mike Clark to get it organized and be its first executive director. He eventually declined, which led to the establishment of a more representative steering committee the next year, again with a first-year's budget raised outside of ATR's own funding. What transpired thereafter is fully reported in an excellent history that Western States Center commissioned to cover its first ten years. Written by Eileen Shaw and entitled *Decade of*

Change 1987–1997, it is the source of the excerpts below and served as a check on my own memories, for I had the pleasure of serving as chair of the steering committee and the founding board. Shaw writes:

> *The Committee included ATR activists Dave Bockmann, Mary Brumder, Anne Knight, Alan and Andrea Rabinowitz as well as Cynthia Guyer, director of the Youth Project Western Office, Cary Schaye, organizer for the United Mine Workers Union, Howard Shapiro, media consultant, Gail Stolz, director of the Montana Democratic Party, Mike Clark, director of the Environmental Policy Institute; Bill Mitchell, director of the Northwest Nuclear Safety Campaign; and Guadalupe Guajardo, trainer for the Center for Third World Organizing.*

On the basis of formal interviews after a national search for suitable candidates, the committee selected Jeff Malachowsky, who had worked for many years for the Fair Share citizens' groups in Massachusetts and Oregon and most recently had been drafted to manage a last-minute Democratic campaign for U.S. Senate in Oregon. He was the husband of Cynthia Guyer, who was the Youth Project's western director and also on the ATR board. Portland, Oregon, where Jeff and Cynthia lived, was designated as headquarters in order to avoid the impression that everything in the ATR context had to be run from Seattle. An early decision was to expand the region by adding Nevada, Utah, and Alaska to the mix because those three states were notably lacking in progressive, community-based organizations; the result was an eight-state region compared to ATR's five-state range.

Jeff, as had been hoped, provided solid leadership. He and Cynthia also did most of the fundraising in the early years, attracting significant contributions from major foundations across the country (and always never enough from individuals). At the beginning, in January 1987, the Youth Project was the Center's fiscal agent; later a separate, tax-exempt corporation was set up. Malachowsky also provided some of the Center's favorite mottos: "Riding the range for social change" and "Working to build the progressive movement in the West." Shaw noted the steering committee's emphasis on the importance of electoral politics and on the interconnectedness of social change activities across the region, and wrote:

> *Malachowsky embarked on year-long outreach and consultation process to activists within the region including community organizers, state representatives, progressive journalists, labor and political leaders, and educators as well as regional centers in other parts of the country.*
>
> *Based on these interviews, Western States Center adopted a strategy of supporting groups developing work in three primary areas: grassroots and community organizing; permanent progressive statewide coalitions; and progressive electoral strategies. The organization also pursued exploratory steps in several other areas including a regional benefits program as a contribution towards staff stability; a network of progressive public officials; and a cultural organizing project.*
>
> *The fundamental objectives of the Center, however,*

far exceeded the bounds of specific issues or project areas. They included:

- *creating an infrastructure to sustain and develop a regional progressive movement;*
- *challenging political and geographic isolation; and*
- *creating opportunities for collective analysis and reflection.*

The Center's first three years were characterized by gathering information and building relationships with progressive leaders and activists throughout the eight states of its region. The Center's constituency covered 13 million people spread across 1.3 million square miles. During these years, Western States concentrated on building credibility and close working relationships with key leaders across this vast area.

Decade of Change 1987–1997 appeared quite soon after Dan Petegorsky left the Peace Development Fund and became the Center's second and equally dynamic executive director. In the book, Aileen Shaw describes in considerable detail how the various programs and activities carried on in that period reflected changing conditions in the nation as the right wing increased its attacks on institutions and customs that had become familiar facets of American society in the previous six or seven decades. The summary below of the changing emphasis of Western States Center's work generally follows her outline.

In the first few years, the major focus was on citizen participation in politics and on the Western Progressive Leadership Network (WPLN), a program to build a network of progressive public officials in each of the eight states who could reinforce each other's

42

efforts at getting progressive laws through the several legislatures. The work on WPLN led ineluctably to satisfyingly successful efforts to create powerful statewide coalitions of progressive organizations that Western States Center had helped to start, such as Nevada's Progressive Leadership Alliance (PLAN) and Wyoming's Equality State Policy Center. A related program was designed to strengthen the low-income, ethnic, and community organizations that would provide constituencies for the progressive legislators, and a serious attempt was made to inspire the work of these grassroots organizations by using "cultural workers" such as Si Kahn and Jane Sapp, both well-known troubadors and community organizers who had worked with Pete Seeger and other great folksingers.

A steady parade of programs with mouth-defying acronyms ensued including CLTP (the Community Leadership Training Program), ALMP (the Advanced Leadership Mentorship Program) and, best of the lot, CSTI (Community Strategic Training Initiative). CSTI has grown from small beginnings to emerge in the 21st century as a weeklong coming together of a rotating collection of some 500 progressive community activists from all of the eight states, with scores of topical workshops presented by specialists from across the nation.

But over these years, and continuing up to the present, the political environment simply turned nasty, beginning with anti-gay and lesbian legislative initiatives in Oregon, with more such attacks appearing regularly in other states. These campaigns overlapped with the deceptively named "wise use" movement that aimed to destroy environmental and land-use planning laws on the books. Much of Western States Center's work was necessarily channeled to creating effective opposition to these initiatives; the result, however, meant fewer resources available for advancing other items on the progressive agenda, especially with regard to eliminating discriminatory policies of all sorts and to empowering disadvantaged groups to organize in their own behalf.

Lastly, Western States Center took leadership of a regional effort to track state-level campaign contributions to political individuals and groups, a program that attracted further financial support from major foundations for the establishment of the National Institute for Money in State Politics, nicknamed the DataShaq.

Such unfortunate changes in the political environment became endemic when the millennium year saw the election of George W. Bush and the hegemony of his Republican party in the three branches of the national government. Obviously these events affected the work of ATR as well, and we turn now to a recent effort by ATR to check on the condition of the progressive movement that both ATR and Western States Center were committed to encouraging. By this time, ATR's name had been changed to Social Justice Fund Northwest, and it was time for another survey of grantees. The results of this new SJFNW-ATR survey were published with the title of *Soundings II* in August 2005, a time when the right wing appeared to be in the saddle across the region, a far cry from the earlier idea that the combination of ATR and Western States Center would go a long way to help the progressives to ride the range in freedom.

Where Mike Clark's *Soundings* of 1985 had reported on how ATR's grantees felt about the grantmaking process and about the viability of different organizing techniques, *Soundings II*'s authors, Leah Henry Tanner and Jack Danger, wanted to find out what was happening to the progressive movement itself.

The job that SJFNW hired them to do eventually involved sixty interviewees selected from 1326 organizations that had applied for grants in the 1999–2004 period. The selection process focused on ensuring an even number of rural and urban organizations, and a representative balance of issues and constituencies. As background they noted that:

> [S]ince its inception in 1978, the Social Justice Fund has granted over $11 million to launch and sustain grassroots organizations promoting democracy, human rights, and racial and economic justice in the Northwest and Northern Rockies. . . . Since 1978 the Social Justice Fund has grown from six to over 400 members, and has increased annual grantmaking from $14,000 to nearly $725,000. More than half of the money awarded annually is in the form of multi-year grants . . .

> .   .   .

> Over the two decades since the first Soundings report was published, the rightward trend of regional and national politics noted in that first report has accelerated. As a result, Washington State saw the loss of affirmative action in 1998. Gay, lesbian, bisexual, and transgendered people through the region have faced relentless attacks on their rights, primarily, though not exclusively, through the mechanism of ballot initiatives. National reforms to welfare are having dire consequences in our largely rural region, especially in states like Oregon, which has the highest child poverty rate in the United States as of this writing.

> .   .   .

> Among the questions presented to survey recipients were: 1) Do you think a progressive movement exists in our region? 2) What are some of the barriers to movement building? 3) What are some of the oppor-

tunities? 4) What strategies are groups using to achieve their missions and goals, and 5) How can the Social Justice Fund be an effective ally in these movement building efforts?

From interviewees' responses, it is clear that those who are doing the work of social justice in this region face tremendous challenges. They are struggling with funding issues, they are understaffed, and the consolidation of rightwing political power is adversely affecting many aspects of their constituents' lives. However, they are not downtrodden by these realities. It is obvious they remain hopeful.

The consultants reported that grantees were confronted with difficult social, political, and economic shifts. The consolidation of the conservative right wing's power affected essentially every aspect of peoples' lives; disadvantaged populations were being severely challenged by the increased disparity between the wealthy and the poor, the concentration of wealth, unbridled capitalism, increased globalization of capital, privatization, and rigid corporate control.

The techniques employed by the right wing to exploit "wedge" issues and to force groups to defend their own turfs (especially in the GLBT communities) made coalition building difficult. The consultants found that:

Close to 90% of project participants essentially agree that a progressive movement exists in our region. There also seems to be a shared definition or description of what a progressive movement looks like. Where disagreement arises is around the health and viability of that movement today.

The grantmaking process goes on regardless of the perceived status of a prospective progressive movement at any point in time, and so the consultants went to considerable length to collect actionable suggestions with regard to funding strategies for SJFNW to consider. Many of the grantees' comments were familiar, such as the need to recognize that the demographic profiles of states like Montana and Wyoming remain more homogenously white than in other states, thus making it difficult to meet "politically correct" standards of diversity that might require that all races, classes, genders, and gender-preferences be represented on a governing board. Two sets of comments quoted from respondents reflect similar operational imperatives:

> Focus more on projects that work and are effective and less on funding PC showpieces that make your white liberal funding base feel less guilty. Don't be so dogmatic about the bottom-up organizing model. Sometimes the grass-tips can be powerful too . . .
>
> .   .   .
>
> Raise and grant more money in the simplest manner possible. Your process, even with the simplified one page process, continues to be one of the hardest. Look at who determines who gets funded – are they well positioned to see where the pulse is and follow that?

The 21st century was already five years old by the time *Soundings II* went to press, and, as described in greater detail below, the original ATR had become a different, larger, more public entity by that time. The next task, in the following chapter, is to show how ATR moved forward from the character it had in the last decade of the 20th century to the present reality of its reformulation as Social Justice Fund Northwest.

Logo for Western States Center

CHAPTER 5

Transmogrification for the 21st century

The two decades between 1985 (when *Soundings I* was published) and 2005 (when *Soundings II* was published) saw the relatively small and relatively homogenous ATR transformed in extraordinary and difficult stages into the Social Justice Fund Northwest we know as this short biography is written. The changes included larger size (at least five times as big); a less exclusionary membership fee; greater racial, class, and gender diversity in both membership and board composition; and a more compelling voice in the philanthropic community of the Northwest.

One price that had to be paid for all this growth was that the larger organization needed more regularized procedures and more professional staff, thus gradually reducing the sense of intimacy for individual members that had characterized the early days at ATR. This final chapter attempts to convey some sense of all that transpired.

Thus far in history, progressive public foundations have not had large endowments, so the primary job of their executive directors has always been to bring in revenue from a membership, in contrast to the job of an executive director in a well-endowed private foundation whose primary assignment is to give the income on the endowment away as adroitly as can be. Since the cost of a full membership in ATR had declined from its original exclusionary $3,500 a year to a more welcoming $20 a month or $240 a year, membership recruitment on a vast, unfamiliar scale became imperative, even though membership from such dues could never provide a goodly sum for giving away in the form of grants.

And so the ebb and flow of revenue is inevitably a central feature of life at a progressive public foundation, and Table 3 is here to provide testimony as to ATR's record on that kind of scoreboard. All the data come from federal income tax returns except for one year when I had to use the audited financial statement for the year. An ocean of detail remains in those dusty archives, but there is not quite enough of it to be able to convey a full understanding of the split between funds received for general granting and administration, for special "outside" funds for designated regrantings, or for additions to the endowment. The column marked "total contributions," however, is a faithful record of monies sent to ATR/SJFNW each year as charitable contributions according to the tax returns.

The column marked "total grants" is also as accurate an accounting as the tax records can provide, but it is not possible to separate out the general grant category from donor-advised or regranting funds. Table 3 suggests a grantmaking capacity somewhat below a million dollars a year, except for several years around the turn into the 21st century when ATR received special funds for regranting, including some grants to be focused on immigration and some on gender problems in society.

TABLE 3. Total contributions and total grants by year, 1978–2004

	Total Contributions, including General, Special, & Endowment ($)	Total Grants ($)
1978	33,086	14,000
1979	63,064	42,403
1980	67,030	30,567
1981	86,807	59,265
1982	157,468	87,343
1983	195,313	152,144
1984	235,640	179,909
1985	248,165	196,950
1986	350,308	201,809
1987	250,357	182,071
1988	250,844	163,970
1989	311,288	226,791
1990	311,809	181,428
1991	391,448	195,998
1992	429,545	234,000
1993	596,043	363,745
1994	741,818	410,887
1995	822,937	462,007
1996	899,974	573,529
1997	1,898,415	1,007,493
1998	2,239,320	937,783
1999	1,296,760	903,903
2000	1,289,346	962,035
2001	1,042,155	554,330
2002	1,168,877	668,926
2003	1,581,962	403,350
2004	1,199,137	723,578

Those high points in contributions to the general fund, plus receipts from the endowment and assorted other sources, came in the last few years of the 20th century, but times were changing. The first years of the 21st century were extremely difficult on all fronts, especially since big donations from major foundations, a feature of the mid-1990s, were not in prospect.

The number of full, associate, and honorary members, plus staff and outside directors and small contributors to the old ATR, probably never exceeded a hundred. To preserve confidentiality, only a few people (those on the fundraising committee, the executive director, and not including me in the many years I served as treasurer) knew which members made the large-sized contributions which were and are necessary to allow ATR's granting program to be significant. Old-timers like me thus marvel at the extraordinary success of the successor generation at Social Justice Fund née ATR in raising useful amounts of money as well as raising membership to new heights. For the year 2005, the fact is that the 632 members contributed $891,000 to the general fund. The socioeconomic-political conundrum that seems intractable is that the 466 members in the minimal-cost membership category were able to contribute only 9 percent of the total while the organization had to rely on an anonymous group of 23 well-off individuals to give an average gift of $24,400 and thus provide 63 percent of the grantmaking monies. It is hard to "build community feeling" under such conditions of unequal financial capacities. Solutions to this imbalance are hard to imagine; the search for them is unending.

Not surprisingly, given the wrenching change from the past to a future that was confronting this awkward interrelationship of finances and racial equity, the administrative staff suffered from high turnover between the time in May 1999 when Carol Pencke left and May 2001 when Bookda Gheisar was appointed as executive director. An enormous and critical burden was carried by the fundraising committee under the leadership of Ivan Inger to get

ATR through this transition period; fortunately the committee was successful in reestablishing a cadre of continuing givers within the region that would provide for a reasonable level of operations under a changed environment for philanthropy in general and social activism in particular. The contributions column in Table 3 reflects the highs and lows of those later years.

The basic transformative changes sketched above mostly came about while Carol Pencke was ATR's executive director. By profession she was a schoolteacher, but she had consummate skill as a fundraiser, a talent honed while she was volunteer national chair of NARAL (National Abortion Rights Action League). Year by year she brought more well-to-do members into ATR; she obtained large financial contributions from distant foundations for special regranting programs; she took the lead in opening up the regional association of foundations to its responsibility to embrace the public foundations that had sprung up; and, of greatest importance to ATR's future, she stage-minded the innumerable meetings and training sessions about "race and class diversity" that were considered a necessary, seemingly interminable, part of a process to assure that the requisite changes would be sufficiently deep and long lasting.

The need for greater diversity had been felt for a long time, but the membership eventually understood that the need could never be met by having a few nonwhite, non-well-to-do board members and staff (and even a few, very few, full-paying nonwhite members), and certainly not by insisting on a level of diversity inside grantee organizations that ATR itself could not equal. And so, about 1993, Gary Delgado, one of the great nonwhite members of the ATR and Western States Center boards in their early years, recommended Susan Colson, a skilled facilitator (and a white woman) to help ATR deal with this whole puzzle in a better way, at a time when almost none of the foundations in the area had even begun to be sensitive to the issue. And one must remember that this was also the time when rightwing leaders were casting and broadcasting aspersions on most of ATR's social goals.

What follows is a characterization of the internal dialogue during the ensuing decade of debate, exploration, experimentation, trainings, reeducation, and overhaul of procedures that went on after the Colson consultations and the manifesto from the summer meeting in Laramie in 1997 that committed ATR to a difficult process of change.

- To even think about attracting a diverse membership, the annual dues must be drastically lowered.

- Lower revenues from dues means that we must have a much larger membership in order to have enough grant funds to make an impact.

- We can't attract such a larger, more diverse, membership unless we have board, staff, and procedures that are welcoming to and supportive of diversified membership.

- All of the above means that the current membership must do its best to eradicate racist thinking and habits in its own group through trainings, etc. (and to maintain financial contributions, or even increase them, while simultaneously creating an endowment).

The emotional stresses resulting from trying to honor such moral imperatives have coursed through the organization in one form or another to the present day. An early step at ATR involved training in order to gain broad acceptance of the concept that really appropriate interpersonal relations between diverse groups requires more than polite "politically correct" (PC) speech and thought. How was one supposed to internalize these ideas instead of merely mouthing nice sentiments? What was the proper word to use, anyhow? Gary Delgado himself told of conflict with his minority organizer-trainees when he used the word "Black" instead of "African American" as they had expected. Gary had to remind them that he had gone to the barricades during the civil rights struggles after World War II in order to be able to substitute "Black" for "Colored." And could a Black use "black" while a white was restricted to using "African American" as a designator? And were any such descriptive terms appropriate in an age when organizations should be color-blind, or was it going to be necessary to rely on affirmative action, practically speaking forever, and could one give equal weight to the claims of those with a variety of gender preferences, national/racial origins, religious practices, or physical limitations; was there, indeed, a "hierarchy of oppressions," that is, my oppression being greater than yours? And so on.

ATR wasn't alone among the "progressive" segments of society in having agonizing times dealing with sometimes angry constituents. For one example, the National Network of Grantmakers, a meeting ground for progressive funders, had come into existence about the same time as ATR and, over the years, spawned a collection of affiliates such as Hispanics in Philanthropy, Native Americans in Philanthropy, Asian-American/Pacific Islanders in Philanthropy, and a score of others for every different ethnic/cultural group, alongside a number of highly focused public and private foundations newly dedicated to environmental, international, GLBT, African American, and any number of other potentially divisive issues about diversity and fairness.

Quite possibly the new generation that has converted ATR into the Social Justice Fund Northwest may not bear the scars of these conflicts about race and gender as did those in the earlier generation that was dominant in ATR in the 1990s, and some issues of class and income are more in the limelight at the present time than issues of race. In any case, ATR was at its twenty-year mark when the pressures for change were rocking the boat, and it all happened on Carol Pencke's watch. Here is her accounting about the transformations going on, excerpted from her piece in ATR's newsletter as we celebrated our organization's 20th anniversary in 1998.

A Territory Resource began as a grand experiment, and not everyone shared David [Hunter]'s confidence. At ATR's inception in 1978, no one had ever considered forming a regional, public foundation whose mission, at its core, was to redistribute wealth and power in America. Few believed that wealthy Americans would voluntarily support organizations which worked to level the playing field that had created that wealth.

There was no concept of the Northwest and Northern Rockies as a region, never mind as a region with widely disparate economic, ethnic and geographical needs. No one noted that, until . . . the advent of the high tech miracle industries and growth of the Pacific Rim trade; our region operated much like a "third world colony" to the rest of the United States. We exported raw materials – timber, water, minerals, agricultural products – and bought them back as finished goods. With the exception of airplanes and some finished lumber, the region produced virtually no "value-added" products. . . .

The annual summer meeting of members, board and staff became a mainstay, and long, long work sessions throughout the year became the norm. Confidentiality was still important, but members at least knew each other's last names and developed an in-house mailing list. . . .

Growth raised a question: it was happening, but was it good? In the middle years – our youth – ATR grew slowly and developed new policies. . . . The Cultural Grants cycle was born. What began as a $2,000 fund has reached $40,000 and is the most popular granting committee within the foundation.

ATR also began to look more closely at itself. Do we mirror what we ask of the region? Board members took the lead and brought in consultants to work with the Board, membership and staff on the issue of diversity. As with any self-examination, there were strains and bruised feelings, but also a chance to come together and celebrate. We rewrote the bylaws, blended advisory and donor boards and committees and expanded membership.

We looked at our granting as well. Could we offer larger grants over longer periods to build progressive institutions? The answer was a typical "yes, we can!" and Major Grants began in 1993.

And what about support for ATR? We undertook a focused effort to bring national funds to our region. These efforts began to bear fruit in 1993 when ATR received its first grant from the Public Welfare Foundation to support our Technical Assistance Fund.

What of the last five years? Since 1993, ATR has been on a growth course. Our income grew from

$444,000 in 1992 to a projected $1.5 million in 1997. This includes gifts to the Endowment for the Twenty-first Century, a stabilizing fund with a goal of $2.1 million that will eventually support all of ATR's administrative expenses. Membership grew from 65 to 230 with over 100 other contributors, ATR instituted Donor Advised accounts which in 1997 accounted for 8% of our total. Foundation grants and corporate match funds now provide over 20 percent of our resources. We developed and presented Managing Wealth conferences as a service to members. . . . ATR was recognized in 1995 as the Northwest Outstanding Philanthropic Foundation and received a Community Service Award in 1997.

Carol made available the statistical data I have abstracted in Appendix Two and also produced a long list of ATR's pioneering efforts, from which I have selected a few:

- *ATR provided first grants to Centra Campesino; Northwest Coalition Against Malicious Harassment; The Black Dollar Days Task Force; Native Action; The Nuclear Safety Campaign; Idaho Women' s Network; and the Women's Funding Alliance.*

- *ATR members founded the Western States Center, a regional training, networking, and research center based in Portland, Oregon.*

- *ATR began providing networking and training opportunities for grantees and donors, sponsoring among others: Funders' Briefings on Native Issues; the Nuclear Safety Campaign start-up meetings; Democracy under Siege; Philanthropy*

*in the Next Millennium; and, the Northwest Immigrant
Safety Net.*

. . .

*Serving as the Director of this institution is a great honor.
When I look ahead, I still wonder if we can ever reach a funding level that challenges the resources garnered by our oppor-
tunity, or that matches the needs of our region. That goal still
lies out of our reach. Nonetheless, I congratulate our loyal
supporters of the first two decades. I look forward with great
excitement to the next 10 years. David [Hunter], I wonder
what you will say then?!*

ATR was a unique resource for its five-state territory in its early
years, especially in the excitingly novel way it enabled a
donor/grantor to work directly with a donee/grantee. A colleague
in this work was the McKenzie River Gathering (MRG), a member
of the Funding Exchange but dedicated to the opposite practice of
separating donors from the actual grantmaking function, which
was to be operated by "community members." MRG, with the support of ATR, tried to expand out of its primary range of Oregon
into the Seattle area in the mid-nineteen-nineties to attract progressive donors willing to contribute smaller sums than were then
required for membership in ATR but met with only moderate success, as was also true when MRG created the Common Wealth Fund
in its image to do a better job of combing the market in Washington
State; Common Wealth elected to close up shop in November 1985.

Eventually ATR as a progressive public foundation was joined
by some new ones, notably the Pride Foundation started by gays
and lesbians that has operated in an increasingly impressive way
since it opened, and Social Venture Partners (SVP, technically a
fund at the Seattle Foundation), founded by a group of newly

wealthy high-tech moguls to provide a philanthropic home and training ground for the similarly privileged young millionaires being created in the Seattle area. SVP has adopted a philosophy that encourages its members to find some way of working as volunteers for the organizations it funds, so that its geographic range is restricted to the immediate area which keeps it from being the kind of regional resource that ATR set out to be. On the other hand, the local SVP group has introduced its SVP model to like-minded folk in a score of other cities around the United States (and a few other countries), so that the Seattle group is now in partnership with its new sister organizations around the nation and the globe. Also joining the progressive front of the 1990s locally were the western office of the Peace Development Fund and church-related groups, primarily the Campaign for Human Development (created by the Catholic bishops after the assassination of Martin Luther King) and a number of Catholic sisterhoods.

While the foundation world became somewhat more open and responsive nationally during the latter years of the 20th century, Seattle's leadership took its time learning about social responsibility and the importance of participation in the public arena by the kind of grassroots groups funded by innovative foundations like ATR. The question in the 1980s took the form of whether such charitable organizations could become members of the regional association of grantmakers, then known as the Pacific Northwest Grantmakers Forum (PNGF), now reconstituted as Philanthropy Northwest. At that time, however, the philanthropic community in Seattle was extremely narrow. Then it was composed of one large community foundation, a few grantmaking arms of the dominant corporations such as Boeing and Weyerhaeuser (Microsoft did not yet exist), a few family foundations (such as Bullitt, Medina, Nesholm, Kreielsheimer, and Skinner), and the United Way. So that was more or less the culture of the town when PNGF was started and became the regional affiliate of the national Council on Foundations. Each of the charter members of PNGF was funded by a single "reliable" source with the notable exception of the Seattle Foundation, the local community foundation founded in 1946, a tax-exempt organization supported by a considerable number of donors who were established local citizens. A foundation like the Seattle Foundation would later be defined in the great Tax Act of 1969 as a "public foundation."

Perhaps because ATR was seen as a foundation for young people of some individual wealth, it had been allowed to become a member of the Pacific Northwest Grantmakers Forum long before other public foundations were invited in. Nationally some public foundations, led by the Tides Foundation in San Francisco, were trying to get the Council on Foundations to accept the new social-change public foundations as members. Locally ATR's executive director Carol Pencke took leadership of a small group (calling ourselves the Northwest Association of Progressive Grantmakers), that was ultimately successful in helping to open up PNGF to the broader range of socially active public foundations listed above, beginning with the Pride Foundation and the Catholic Church's Campaign for Human Development.

ATR members were also involved in a successful campaign to permit progressive funders, such as the ones at ATR, to become members in the progressive National Network of Grantmakers, originally a meeting place for minority program officers and executive directors of large foundations who were trying to get their foundations to make social-change grants.

The philanthropic scene at the turn of the century continued to be involved with internal changes of the kind that ATR was going through in order to deal responsibly with all the demands and issues around diversity and affirmative action, but at the same time, all across the country, foundations, charitable individuals, and all the institutions and organizations that wanted their money were licking their wounds from the collapse of the dot.com stock market. The 9/11/01 event has merely exacerbated the pressures on the philanthropic system. Many funders had reduced their grantmaking to such an extent that grantees were suffering withdrawal symptoms from the loss of their major supporters. Social change grantees were particularly affected. New tax-exempt organizations for all sorts of causes emerged at the end of the 20th century and wanted their share of funding; the 1996 Welfare Reform Act, for example, spurred the creation of many protective and advocacy groups in the context of the work of United for a Fair Economy in popularizing "popular economics" and providing clear evidence of the growing disparity between rich and poor.

One initiative for reform of the philanthropic system in America called for a mandatory increase in the percentage of a foundation's endowment to be paid out to grantees each year, and for exclusion of administrative costs incurred by the foundation for (fancy) offices, (fancy) salaries, and (fancy) board meetings. The world of more traditional philanthropic community naturally resisted these ideas for reform.

The most dramatic change, however, was the increased sense that our society was being dominated by the very large concentration of power, marginalizing all the efforts of progressives interested in social change. And then came the new breed of supersized foundations. The foundation established by Microsoft's Bill Gates, for example, had to make grants amounting to more than one billion dollars a year, far more than all the progressive foundations in the nation combined. The progressive voice was being systematically excluded as media became concentrated in conservative hands. The onslaught of the right wing on civil liberties, on welfare programs and environmental protections, and even on the premises for progressive philanthropy, increased both the demand for help from progressive foundations and the difficulty in selecting grantees among the multitude of proposals.

There is no doubt that progressive activist organizations and progressive foundations are always challenged by questions about their effectiveness and their survivability, and never more so than at the present time, in this era of gigantism. How donors and their grantees will fare in this 21st century is something that only time will tell. Perhaps some will take comfort from this little history, gaining some perspective on what transpired in the last few decades of the now-remote 20th century, and perhaps some encouragement that creative work on a small scale in the field is still possible.

I think it is appropriate to let Max Milton, one of ATR's founders, provide the capstone to our work. He is a writer and poet, environmentalist, a staunch Montanan, and an environmentally savvy rancher devoted to the region that stretches from the Northern Rockies to the Pacific. And even though he was writing for ATR's 20th anniversary report, much of what he says applies to the present and the foreseeable future for our work.

> *Was our experiment of 20 years ago successful? Yes! The population of the Pacific Northwest has grown from to 2 million to 7.8 million. Funds available for traditional social services have diminished, but funds available to progressive philanthropy have increased. And while the number of qualified organizations and projects competing for those funds has exploded, there is a strong infrastructure of nontraditional philanthropy in place.*

Still, although the region is wealthier than we could have imagined, it is also poorer and more stressed. Social, natural and financial resources are simultaneously thriving and strained. There are, however, a number of stable community organizations producing citizen leaders and influencing public policy and public discussion.

There is ebb and flow as issues and challenges shift. Sometimes there is too close a mirroring of immediate political debate and not enough long-term vision and investment. There continues to be a need to understand how social, natural and financial community wealth are related.

Max is just one of the multitude (many score and maybe more than a hundred) of individualistic characters who were part of this goodmoney collective in its first years, and I regret that I did not find a way, as I wrote this little book, to recognize and appreciate what each contributed at that time to our sense of being a healthy, creative, functional, and unique community. We have scattered, a few have died, a number of the couples split, the original batch of kids has grown, but friendships have lasted, and many have continued to lead constructive and even distinguished lives. I think most of us would agree with the rousing sentiment with which Max ended his piece.

To educate broadly about how all our actions affect each other and the world, there continues to be a need for groups of caring individuals to learn to trust each other and work together to honor heart and

mind equally, and to strive to build our communities
with intention.

These words, though written in 1998, epitomize the intimate spirit with which ATR began and which characterizes all that has transpired and that will, I trust, guide the present and foreseeable future efforts of the Social Change Fund Northwest and the Western States Center, those worthy descendants of our ATR.

. . .

The People of ATR

Lisa Tremaine, then at the Social Justice Fund Northwest office, was kind enough to compile the lists below, which I have supplemented slightly with information from the IRS 990 tax returns.

DIRECTORS The directors are listed alphabetically within five-year ranges that reflect the dates when their terms seem to have begun, with undoubtedly some mistakes of omission and commission; the information on when their years of service ended was less comprehensive and thus is not shown. The letter "P" in brackets after a name indicates that the individual served at some point and for some years as president (or latterly, chair) of the board; a "T" in brackets indicates service as treasurer.

1978–82

Booth, Heather
Brumder, Mary [P]
Charter, Jeanne
Clerc, Kim
Fox, Michael [T]

Guajardo, Guadalupe
Hancock, Loni
Hunter, Barbara
Hunter, David
Mitchell, Bill

1983–87

Blyberg, Ann
Bockman, John
Caine, Lynda
Guyer, Cynthia [P]

Harris, Margie
Lamson, Joe
Mowat, Greg
Thomas, Karen

1988–92

Brummel, Jack [P]
Brunton, Beth
Colson, Susan
Delgado, Gary
Edison, Suzanne [P]
Elmer, Don
Ferguson, Ellen
Ferrel, Cipriano
Gillespie, Cynthia
Ito, Alice
Miller, Whitney
Milton, Max

Mize, Anne [P]
Narasaki, Diane
Pencke, Michael [T]
Rabinowitz, Alan [T]
Russell-Alexander, Yolanda
Sandusky, Gary
Shapiro, Howard
Styles, Hurdie
Teichman, Ebo
Titcomb, Peter [T]
Wiener, Sara

1993–97

Becker, Jim [T]
Bocanegra, Juan [T]
Crawford, Kathleen
Dayton, Lucy [P]
Foecke, David [T]
Gamble, Helen
Gonzales, Adeline
Goode, Paul
Harris, Glenn
Jung, Soya

Klein, Kim
Kunreuther, Robert
Liebman, Becky
McKay, Karen
Miller, Julie
Petitt, Kimberly
Simons, Ron [T]
Smith, Patrick
Tobin, Judy [P]
White, Ron

1998–2002

Adams, Neil

Arnow, Jill [P]

Baker, Michael [T]

Becker, Barbara

Bratton, Rosemary

Close, Gracie (Pat) [P]

Hale, Sandy

Hernandez, Marta

Himes, Andy

Inger, Ivan

Kaplan, Victoria

Kleinman, Larry [P]

Kurose-Woo, Marie

Lemus, Vince

Merrill, Liz

Owens, Garry

Ponder, Melissa

Rabinowitz, Andrea

Robideau, Janet

Smith, Eric [T]

Ward, Eric

Wise, Tim

2003–06

Becker, Jim

Blanford, Stephan

Bowman, Moira [T]

Brumder, Mary

Flora, Lydia

Gonzalez, Felicia

Goodwin, Vickie

Kaplan, Victoria [T]

Lamberjack, Natalie

Leonard, John

McKinney, Lora-Ellen

Schwan, Bryony

Villarosa, Lori

Yasinski, Nick

HONOREES

Lisa Tremaine's note: *I looked these up recently for Bookda, but only found the names of those for 2001 and prior for the David Hunter award and 2000 and prior for the Jeanette Rankin award. They are listed below.*

My note: Another study not quite as long as this history of ATR would be required to provide a satisfactory description of the lives of these honored individuals and of how they had been and are of service to ATR or the region; thus a possible part of somebody else's manuscript appears.

THE DAVID R. HUNTER AWARD was given annually to an ATR member who had devoted long-term service to the foundation and its work. The award was named to honor an ATR founder, lifelong community activist, and former Director of the Stern Family Fund and the Ottinger Foundation. David based his career on creating progressive, collaborative philanthropy. Recipients from 2001 and prior include:

- ATR's Founders: Anonymous, Heather Booth, Christopher L. Boyd, Mary Brumder, Jill Bullitt, David R. Hunter, Maxwell Milton, William Mitchell, Connie M. Staudohar and Eberhard Teichmann

- Alan and Andrea Rabinowitz

- Peter Titcomb

- Ellen Ferguson

- Judy Tobin

- Julie Miller

- Pat Close and David Foecke

Lisa Tremaine's note: *In 2002 the nominees were: Larry Kleinman, Barbara and Jim Becker, and Alice Ito. I don't know who actually received the award that year.*

My note: Each of those listed by Lisa had worked with devotion for ATR. The award, which had been in abeyance, was resurrected in 2006, renamed the Hunter-Pious Award to recognize the contributions of the late Connie Pious, and was presented to Becky Liebman at the annual dinner.

THE JEANETTE RANKIN AWARD is given annually to a lifelong activist who has served the ATR-SJF region of Idaho, Montana, Wyoming, Washington, and Oregon. This award embodies the hard work, dedication, and strong spirit of the community activist. The award is named in honor of the first woman to serve in Congress, from the state of Montana, who served as a community organizer, labor activist, and lifelong peace activist. The recipient receives a $1,000 cash prize. In 2006 the award was given to Rosalinda Guillen.

Recipients from 2000 and prior include:

- Teresa Erickson
- Juan Bocanegra
- Suzanne Pharr
- Gail Small
- Gary Sundusky
- Rosemary Bratton

EXECUTIVE DIRECTORS

- Greg Caplan'Tuke (approximately 1978–84)
- David Bockmann
- Nora Hallett
- Valerie Reuther
- Eunice Letzing
- Carol Pencke (approximately 1991–May 1999)
- Barbara Green (acting)
- Janis Strout
- Bookda Gheisar (May 2001 to date)

ATR's first twenty years of grantmaking

Appendix Two is a rendition of the revealing statistics that Carol Pencke presented in the ATR 20th anniversary report. The data give a sense of what ATR grants were designed to accomplish during the first twenty-two years, 1978 through 1990. The text is my analysis and commentary.

Table 4 takes the total amount of the grants for the 1978–1990 period and shows how much was allocated to each of the five states in the ATR region. Table 5 shows how much was allocated to the various types of issues, and Table 6 sheds light on the kinds of strategies that were used by the grantees in their attempts to effect change. The Miscellaneous entry in Table 4 mostly refers to grants that cover more than one state.

TABLE 4. Total amount granted per state, 1978–1990

State	Amount	No. of groups
Washington	593,941	80
Oregon	360,365	47
Montana	340,705	32
Idaho	155,944	16
Wyoming	50,395	5
Miscellaneous	121,239	
TOTAL	1,622,580	

The entries in Table 5 constitute a catalogue of what is meant by social change philanthropy at work. One of the fixations of progressive grantmakers at the end of the 20th century was the citizen-based organization that tried to build statewide political strength by tackling whatever social or economic issue was important at any particular time in any particular locality, and often by building a temporary coalition of groups interested in a particular issue; grants to such groups come under the Multi-issue heading. ATR took some leadership in bringing anti-AIDS groups together, and this work is reflected in the Health/Act Up category. The other categories are self-explanatory.

TABLE 5. Issues funded, 1978–1990

Issue	Amount
Multi-issue	397,390
Environmental/Natural resources	186,761
Peace/Disarmament	128,322
Women's Rights/Lesbians	125,064
Rural/Hispanic farmworkers	95,838
Intermediate TA providers	79,648
Alternative energy/nuclear power	78,500
Central American policy	75,143
Native American	65,937
Low-income/Welfare/Housing	57,306
Health/Act Up	27,259
Labor/Jobs	16,988
Voter registration/Immigration	15,650
Senior issues	12,000
Anti-hate groups	10,000
Children's/Youth issues	7,000

Another fixation on the part of progressive grantmakers in that period was "community organization," which in Table 6 is represented to have absorbed the largest share of grant funds. At one end of the spectrum of preferred organizing strategies was the kind of activism famously developed by Saul Alinsky in the Chicago area; that form relied primarily on participation by church congregations on behalf of disadvantaged populations. All sorts of less dramatic forms of organizing at the grassroots level are found at the other end, including Fair Share, "low-income coalitions," and organizing of low-income jobholders by unions. Carol Pencke had some further explanations in her report:

> *Obviously, most groups use a variety of strategies in their work. I met with past ATR directors and we reviewed the computer printout of all grants, and tried to designate the* primary *strategy used by each organization. In several cases involving legislation we assigned half the grant dollars to a legislative strategy and half to the other key strategy, either organizing – or public education. Examples include: Idaho Conservation League (legislation and organizing) and Montana Environmental Information Center (legislation and public education). Public Education refers to those groups who are primarily getting the word out and educating the general public on an issue, rather than organizing a membership constituency.*

TABLE 6. Strategies funded, 1978–1990

Strategy	Amount
Community organizing	744,146
Public education	210,601
Coalition development	135,980
Legislative	116,340
Training by intermediaries	78,148
Voter registration	14,650
Economic development	11,000
Media	10,000
Advocacy	8,400
Model programs	5,000

The grantees Carol named as examples of each of the strategies above are one last bit of evidence of the scope of ATR's interests:

- **Community Organizing:** Idaho Fair Share, Centro Campesino, Montana Low Income Coalition. This also includes institutional organizing such as ILWU Local # 37 and Portland Organizing Project.

- **Public Education:** Center for Democratic Renewal, Hanford Education Action League, Novela Health Foundation

- **Coalition development:** Citizens Alliance for Progressive Action, Montana Alliance for Progressive Policy, Oregon Coalition Project

- **Legislative** (groups with a major goal of organizing/educating their constituencies about legislative issues, *not* direct lobbying): National Abortion Rights Action League, Montana Women's Lobby, Fair Budget Action Campaign

- **Training/Intermediary:** Western States Center, Northern Rockies Action Group, Women's Funding Alliance
- **Economic Development:** Puget Sound Development Foundation
- **Media:** Community Marketing & Media Center
- **Advocacy:** Seattle Consumer Action Network
- **Model Programs:** Shoalwater Fuelwood

Social Justice Fund Northwest posts a great deal of information about its various grants programs and its other activities on its Web site: www.socialjusticefund.org. Of special interest are its current definitions of community organizing. Readers can reach them at 603 Stewart Street, Suite 1007, Seattle WA 98101-1229; telephone (206) 624-4081; fax (206) 382-2640.

Some thoughts by Bookda Gheisar, Executive Director of Social Justice Fund Northwest from 2001 to the present

I am privileged to be an integral part of the amazing organization whose origins are so crisply and interestingly presented in this little book. We will make good use of this long-wanted history.

The book does a good job of describing how ATR, after its first quarter-century of pioneering, needed to change in order to be a more useful partner in the progressive movement of the Northwest that we have been funding. In the last few years, as we collectively try to craft a cogent regional organizing strategy, we have done the best we know how to reach out to the wide array of stakeholders in the region in order to build a membership base broad enough to incorporate an understandably diverse set of perspectives. We have been building an organization that transcends race and class, and one that brings both money and these differing perspectives to the decision-making table.

Since its inception, the relatively well-to-do members of the foundation had been concerned by the paucity of members of color and people of the middle and working classes, the very groups they sought social justice for. By the end of the 20th century, it became clear to all of us that this was an insidious form of institutional racism and that we could do (and had to do) something about it.

As this book notes, the face of our membership has changed dramatically since 2002 when we lowered the annual cost of membership. Now included, as hoped, are the longtime activists, middle-class professionals, and grassroots social-change activists who had never before seen themselves as philanthropists, sitting at the table with wealthy donors as equal partners. And then, at a time when so many rights are under attack, a more appropriate name was needed to increase our ability to raise and grant funds, so we changed our name from ATR/A Territory Resource Foundation to Social Justice Fund Northwest to make it even more clear who we are and to express our politics more overtly.

We could not have done all of this without the great work, great wisdom, tremendous vision, and wonderful values of the people who have participated throughout ATR's history, especially the founders. We are building upon their legacy—both in values and vision, and in the internal infrastructure and in the external relationships they built. One of our great challenges today is to keep the kind of people who created the foundation actively engaged as we continue to add more hundreds (or thousands) of ordinary people—activists, workers, people from all walks of life—who can together create a new vision of social change philanthropy for the new millenium. We see ourselves continuing as a vital source of funding but also as being a reformist instrumentality within mainstream philanthropy, and not the least of that vision is our goal of making philanthropists of everyone who might have the desire to create a better world and be willing to invest just a little (or much) money to help make that better world a reality.